A Slice Of Life

Edited by

Steve Twelvetree

First published in Great Britain in 2005 by
ANCHOR BOOKS
Remus House,
Coltsfoot Drive,
Peterborough, PE2 9JX
Telephone (01733) 898102

SB ISBN 1 84418 396 3

FOREWORD

Anchor Books is a small press, established in 1992, with the aim of promoting readable poetry to as wide an audience as possible.

We hope to establish an outlet for writers of poetry who may have struggled to see their work in print.

The poems presented here have been selected from many entries, and as always editing proved to be a difficult task.

I trust this selection will delight and please the authors and all those who enjoy reading poetry.

Steve Twelvetree
Editor

CONTENTS

A MOTHER'S LOVE

A mother's love begins before we are even born
her bond starts so deep within her heart.
When we are slowly growing within her womb
this is not something anyone of us should take for granted, I presume!

So always remember your mother's love, whether she is here
on Earth or up in Heaven above.
'Cause your mother's love is certainly a gift from God above.

The love your mother gives you never dies 'cause it's
deep within your heart
and this is one thing no man or woman could ever take
or tear apart.

As we begin to grow, we recognise our mother's love
begins to show
'Cause when we're a child, we think like a child and we grow
our love begins to grow and show.
So never hold back in fear the love your received from your
mother's heart throughout the years.

Shout with joy if you ever become a mother, whether it's
a girl or a boy
and never take for granted that beautiful gift of a child.
'Cause there are many people out there who have been trying for
a while, for that lovely gift of a child.

They may bring you laughter, joy, fear and tears, but
always remember your mother's love will
be with you all your years.

When you feel down and sad, just look so deep within your heart,
and sweet memories that your mother shared each week
will put that special smile back on your cheek.

'cause if your mother is now up above
she wouldn't want you to be sad or even think
you've lost her love.

Anastasia Williams Cowper

THE WATERFALL

Hiding behind the waterfall
Too scared to take the leap
All her friends has made it
Why did it look so steep?

The rhythm of the cascade
As it hit the rocks
Was sending out waves
And terrifying shocks

She tried to get her courage
As another passed her by
One leap, two leaps, fall back
She heard the cry

The broken spine was taken
It floated on the crest
What a way to live a life
Just trying to pass this test

She summoned up all she had
Made her gills go slack
Swam towards the waterfall
Without even looking back

Every ounce of energy
Heart banging in her chest
Mussels flexed, tail straight out
She tried to take the test

Cold water slammed her back down again
Against the rocks beneath
She tasted blood
Her body raw
The river had sharp teeth

Totally exhausted, she made one final try
It was as if God gave her wings
She was lifted towards the sky

Almost in slow motion
She was raised above the fall
Maybe only a wild salmon
But she had performed a final curtain call

Jennifer Steddy

IS IT ME?

Am I so bad that I drive them to drink?
This is what I'm beginning to think.

They all need alcohol to help them survive
Not just one, more like four or five.

A can of Fosters? No, got to be stronger!
At least five per cent and one that lasts longer.

What has alcohol got that I can't provide?
Or do they just use it so they can hide?

How can I help if I don't understand?
Do I just bury my head in the sand?

Do I just bear the brunt all the time?
How do I help this love of mine?

I stand tall and I take whatever they throw
It's not them, it's the alcohol, this I know.

I help in a way that I think is best
I move aside and leave them to rest.

But who helps me with this pain -
Do I need alcohol to keep me sane?

Maybe if I drank too, I'd understand
How people you love, become the damned.

She is my lover, my best friend
It is my enemy, will it ever end?

Joanne Patchett

To My Ex-Best Friend

Do you think you can hurt me?
Do you think lying about me makes me sad?
But I'm happier now,
Now I can see through you,
That goes for the rest of your 'friends' too.
We were a family,
We were going to be friends forever,
But now you prefer to back-stab me,
And laugh at me when you can.
You go around with your innocent eyes,
But I can see they're just a glaze.
Do you ever mean what you say?
Don't stop gossiping on my account,
As you need some followers too,
But just remember some day, you'll be hurt too.
Will you rely on those who betrayed me?
I sure hope you do.
Do you know what it feels like -
To be the one blocked out by the wall?
But someday you'll realise that the wall traps you
And that there's no one there at all.
So laugh whilst you can
All I hear is the cackling of your rotting soul.

Claire Begley

COT DEATH

My child died some time ago
As a mum, I did my best
I lay my little child in his cot
To give him a deserved rest.

When I went to get him in the morning
He was an awful colour of blue
I could see he wasn't breathing
And I didn't know what to do.

So I phoned 999, the ambulance came as fast as it could
The paramedics did what they had to do
And the necessary things they should.

Now the paramedic turned and looked at me
As he shook his head,
'I'm sorry I have to tell you Ma'am, but your child was already dead.'

Now my child is in Heaven with our God above
I can speak to him when I pray and also send my love.

John Arthur Williams

UNDERCURRENTS

Undercurrents take me by surprise,
Calm on top, that's the disguise.
What to expect? I don't know!
The brave face is all for show.
Give me a chance, give me a clue,
Tell me what the hell I should do.

Bring me in, help me out,
All the tension makes me shout.
Angry, betrayed, jealous and scared,
As if you think I hadn't cared.
Cry with me as well as them,
Calm down, chill out, count one to ten.

F***k me, it's hard to stay on top,
Of all the s***t that seems to drop!
A break, a change, let's get away,
The pain, the ache, it's not to stay.
Come on, lie down, relax some more,
Move on, forget and close the door.

From the depths, we float again,
God knows why, there are better men.
You stick with me through thick and thin,
Just think, one day, next of kin.
Imagine it now, in years to come,
The undercurrents, they're all gone.

Richard J Smith

MY ESTRANGED CHILDREN

The thoughts of you surround me as I live from day to day
I need another outlet, I hear friendly people say
Though I am just a person and what I am for sure
Is missing you completely, like a frame without a door

My love for you will always be a love I can't implore
The depressing will of someone who deprived me once before
So I travel on to see if I can manage to be free
To get myself amongst some other caring family

I will grow strong just with the thought of seeing you one day
To answer all the questions that you must have tucked away
I know you have grown up now but it seems like yesterday
Your mother and I had to split up and go separately astray

The years have flown right by me, like a bird upon the wing
I've thought of you whenever I've heard a little swallow sing
The love of life has passed me by, though the reason can only be
The knowledge I have inside my heart that you are not with me

And so these feelings I live with have had me in a spin
There's nothing anyone can do to mend my shattered heart again
For it is fully broken and the hurt shows more and more
Without the ones we really love, what is our devotion for?

S C Matthews

REJECTS

Somewhere the sun is shining, with warmth within the air
But a poor soul is pining as her husband is not there
A lonely, simple woman, unhappy on her own
As her children's daddy has left her all alone
He did once serve his nation - now caught up in a 'war'
There should be some elation - that's what she'd been hoping for
Their father was out there searching, but did know very well
That with the constant 'hurting', this Christmas would be hell
No one to bring them presents, to bring about some joy
The locals called them 'peasants' and no one would them employ
Suddenly there was warming, a glow within the room
Her heartbeat then was stalling, there was someone in the gloom
A sort of apparition which to her then did say . . .
'You deserve some true attrition, to drive your fears away
I am here before you, while you're without your man
Someone must adore you, as I am your Samaritan
I have outside a trailer, with provisions for you all
Forget about the rancour, that is what does appall
Out there the louts are banding as you do know well
They need some understanding to stop Christmas being hell
Forget the past I implore you, there'll be peace there in the end
I too do adore you and I will be your constant friend
You are just simple people who only wish to live
Get a grip on what you do - perhaps one day to forgive
Forced into immigration to help your family
I hope I've brought some inspiration to enjoy this Christmas Day
Some hate your infiltration, they think they own this land
One day a new generation, may learn to understand!'

Jackdaw

PENNY

There is a lady in my life
Who is a woman most fine
You think of a person
Made of honesty and wine.

She sees me each morning
As each day is dawning
And the walk she takes
Just leaves me with the shakes.

She knows of most things
And I do agree
With the news that morn' brings
She tells it to me.

I walk the green beside her
But nobody, even I, does she pamper
The friends she brings, can they scamper
A hard life she has known
She works hard with never a moan.

She is a beauty to be seen
Never, nay never, a has been
The short time I've known her
I have to say, if I may

I will be meek, with tongue in cheek
For if I was younger and on this day
I would say, with me, will you come out to play
And with words so true, I'll utter to you, 'My lady,
My lady, I love you.'

Frank Baggaley

LYING FOOD

Lies can be little,
Lies can be big,
Lies can be pork pies,
Lies can be figs,
Lies can be tea,
Lies can be coffee,
Lies can be chocolate,
Lies can be toffee,
Lies can be turkey,
Lies can be chicken,
Lies can be sauce,
To dip your chips in.

Carol Smith (11)

FOREVER IN MY HEART

You were taken away
It all happened so fast
I'm sorry I never said goodbye
My sorrow will always last
Your smile lit up the room
Your laugh leaves fond memories
Why aren't you here anymore?
My life brought to my knees
When we were together
Our love moved Heaven and Earth
Without your very presence
My life has little worth
Now that you're no longer here
And now that we're apart
No one will replace you
You're forever in my heart.

Sarah Streeter

YOU SAY GOODNIGHT

Think of me each night
As you look out of your window
And see those stars
Shining there so bright

Promise to keep a place for me
So close to your heart
Then in love we're not so far apart.

As to the moon and stars
You say goodnight

And as you say a prayer
Remember all of those
Who can't be there

All of those who are so far
Apart tonight

Promise to keep a place for them
So close to your heart

As to the moon and stars
You say goodnight.

K Lake

ONE TO ONE

Needed to make that urgent phone call,
All one got was three options, that's all.
Chose number one, then had to pick from another few,
I still had to wait a moment or two.

After twenty minutes I eventually got through,
Only to find I had to wait in another queue.
By the time I got to the company, they were closed and gone,
Oh, whatever happened to a person and that one to one?

Brenda Wedge

LOVELY HONEYSUCKLE

Oh, my lovely honeysuckle,
How beautiful you are,
First you are a purest white,
Then change to a golden star,
In my garden you are welcome,
Across the lawn you shine,
To see you in the morning,
Helps to make my day sublime.

Accompanied by geraniums red,
That grow beneath your feet.
How they look to adore you.
Your smile is ever sweet.
I know you'll go when winter comes,
But I will patiently wait,
Till you return and say to me,
'Winter is over. 'Tis time for you to awake.'

Albert E Bird

FORBIDDEN IGNORANCE

Do you never stop to hear the sound
Of the terrified cries all around?
Of the scared and vulnerable, young and old
Of the assertive and confident, mighty and bold.

No one bothers to hear their plight
For fear they'll bring heartache within their sight,
They can't bear to feel another's pain
Or watch their teardrops fall like rain.

So many of us pray, in search of inner peace
But for some, the only way is to make themselves deceased.
They feel their life is over, and believe they have no other choice
If only they'd tried harder,
Someone might have heard their crying voice.

Louise Pamela Webster

WHAT DO YOU WANT FOR TEA LOVE?

I've mended his work jeans
Put them on the chair, back where he can't fail to see
Wonder if he notices me?
Monday again, money's tight
The kids get school dinners, so that's alright
Wish we had a jam-packed fridge
Wow, Ready Steady Cook, gorgeous Sean Bean did
For him, I'd bake cider apple pie, whisky, jelly
Triple, ripple, nipple chocolate cake
Dreaming right, fight the diet
Colin's late
Wonder if he still sees her on the quiet
Toast the bread ready, stir the beans
Want to cover his shirt in squirty cream
Tease it down in swirling, laughing trails
Cover him in soft chocolate swirls etched by immaculate nails

Like in a film, well I can dream
Click, ker chuch key in lock, he's back from his garage
I'm hovering by the stove, switched on to marriage,
'Hello Duck, don't wait up, what's all this grub?
It's darts and free sarnies, I'm off to the pub.'

S M Woodbine

GRAVEYARD IN THE SEA

The fear on the old man's face
Clinging onto a tree
Freak of nature
God's choice, God's place
Graveyard in the sea
The world stood still for a second
As the wave crashed onto the land
I watched as the old guy finally gave in
Could no longer hold onto the branch with his frail, bloodied hand

His body lost in the murky water
I could hear a cry out from his daughter
Hysterical she called 'Dad' as she cried
Felt sorry for her seeing her daddy die
Deckchairs and tables floating like toys
Dead are thousands of men, women, girls and boys
Tourists on holiday
Locals and people from afar
Watched as the wave took away a family trying to escape from their car

So many taken
In such a short time
Bodies, oh so many
Taken away on the tide
This is not another 9/11
This is not another war
This is a freak of nature
God, why?
What the hell for?

There must have been a reason
For him to let this be
No one will ever know
Why that wave came crashing out of the sea
Lessons will be taught
Memories will never be gone
Ghosts crying out, please save us
Praying to the setting sun

I would say, 'God bless to you all,'
What's the point when he failed you all?

Stephen A Owen

THE REAL FATHER CHRISTMAS

The toy shop window, brightly lit
Glowing with many a tempting treat
One winter's night, near Christmas
As I stood pondering deep

It was then I noticed, standing near
With flat cap on his head
Another Father Christmas
And to myself I said,

He's dreaming of his children
And thinking for their sake
Just how much money he can spare
To make them happy when they wake.

I, too, was torn between my heart
And financial reality, but
Fathers are not just for Christmas
And love is the brightest tree

I remember that man from years ago
How my heart reached out to him then,
His face bathed in the window light,
He was love, he was peace, he was men.

Joseph McGarraghy

IF ONLY WE HAD A CHOICE

Whether you're a woman or man, or maybe an in-between
It doesn't really matter what you are, you are still a human being.

Most of us are quite lucky cos we fit in with the crowd
Whilst some of us are so lonely we often cry out loud.

We want so much to be accepted and get on with our life
But all we get is mental abuse, misery, torment and strife.

If we could choose our gender, the problem would never arise
We wouldn't go around pretending and never need a disguise.

It's only society that chooses our dress and tells us what to wear
It's fashion that makes men shave their heads and women
                                                    to have long hair.

We all have the same kind of feelings and also a heart that can break
Some of us are weaker than others and sometimes it's more
                                                    than we can take

So please be kind to your fellow man and never make them cry
Remember, but for the grace of God, there goes you or I.

Pauline Mayoh-Wild

FOUNTAIN OF WISDOM

Swimming in a fountain of my own wisdom,
My cheeks glistening with drops of liquid rain,
Living life with my own tranquil fun,
The past is flowing down the drain . . .

As I kiss the stars,
Lapping up the beauty of the night sky,
I hug goodbye to my hidden scars,
And let out a relieved sigh.

Happiness flows through my veins,
I feel like a child on Christmas Eve,
Trying hard to sleep, though it's making me insane,
At the sight of the presents I begin again to breathe.

It's hard to tell where one life ends and another begins,
I have said goodbye to the old me,
I am free, like a bird stretching my glorious wings,
Swimming in my fountain, full of glee.

Kimberly Harries

A CHRISTENING MEMORY

In Thornbury Castle's ancient hall,
Where armour and pike adorn the wall,
Kings and knights have feasted here,
In merriment, with goodly cheer,
At trestled tables on wooden bench,
Served wine by a comely wench.

But today, a different role,
The baptism of an innocent soul,
With happy chatter all around,
Only smiling faces can be found.

Suddenly, above the din,
Resounding from the walls within,
The sound of music, laughter, song,
Celebration by a happy throng,
The lyre strums, the maidens dance,
Around the tables, jesters prance,
Sir Knight did on the table stand,
He raised the chalice in his hand,
'My lords and ladies list' to me,'
Then, ghostly silence instantly,
'A newborn is in the hall, I say,
From a time long past our day.
Let us sup Alexander's health,
Wish him happiness and wealth,'
With goblets raised they supped his name
Wished him long life, health and fame,
Then the ghostly spectres in the hall,
Ebbed back into the ancient wall.

I opened my eyes and glanced around,
Only smiling faces could be found,
Some would say, 'twas just a dream,
But the medieval past, I've seen.

Neil Parkinson

CHRISTMAS AND NEW YEAR

As the months go by and the year draws in,
Festivities arrive, a new year waits to begin,
Christmas trees, decorations, lights, bells and holly,
Spirits are up and people are feeling jolly,
Reflecting on good times, and bad times too,
People suffering from colds and flu!
Children's excitement is rife and contagious,
Adults getting drunk and acting outrageous!
Relationships changing, beginning and ending,
Hope, fear, anticipation of what the new year is sending,
Money worries but happy times, laughter and love,
Everyone nursing a scarf and a glove!
Smiles, tears, sadness, for ones who cannot be near,
With hope in our hearts, we welcome a new year.

Tracy Strain

THE MELD

So tripping through pure beauty read,
in study of that, which past poets said.
Give definition? Fear to tread!
As giving some confuse I said.

And in conclusions I heard poor start,
for the body read had stolen heart,
and rang the words of those great men,
challenges; illusive most to ken.

As with the best comes much eternal,
and owned in manner most paternal,
to take and stir from normal view,
ferment fascination for you.

And should said text be for a rose,
you'll find within deeper repose,
deeper still the works equation,
in the marry melds elation.

Denise K Mitchell

A Last Breath Of Life - Her Thoughts

An ending sigh before her time is past;
she sees her life collapsed upon the ground -
alone and in despair she cannot mask
the need to be remembered; but not found.
Control is lost of all her flying thoughts;
this passing journey, blur to crystal clear.
That hidden memory locked away sought
for in her heart. She flutters a last tear
. . . of joy! She's ready now, let go, release -
a transfer from the Earth to blue beyond.
Her blissful life fulfilled - she rests in peace.
No sight - but her soul never shall be gone.
The eyes of an angel, she looks down through.
She's at my side in all that I may do.

Emily Thommes

A SPECIAL DAY

I was down on my luck
And thought this was the end,
My life was like a broken shell
Which nothing could possibly mend.

As I stood on the river bridge
I thought of the water so deep,
Then I prepared my body
To take a giant leap.

But there came a movement
Out of the mist and fog,
I watched it intently
Till I saw it was a dog.

The little mite was shivering
So I put my coat around,
Then I gently lifted him
Off the sodden ground.

I took him to the police station
Where they gave him food,
To see him looking bright again
Really changed my mood.

The authorities gave me a flat
And my dog came too,
We loved each other's company
As best buddies do.

Scamp rescued me that day
As he came out of the gloom,
For if it hadn't been for him
I would have met my doom.

Rita Hardiman

PRINCESS DARKNESS

I called your name in the middle of the night.
Why do you not come to my desperate plight?
Alone I was and could not see,
I needed you to rescue me.

My darkest hour, this had become.
My judgement day in the barrel of a gun.
Lost in the moment of forever,
I couldn't see light, not now, not ever.

My instinct was all I had with me.
I had to break out, I had to be free.
My spirit soared across the lands.
From the darkness reaching, with outstretched hands.

But all signals were sent back
You are in danger and under attack.
The strength in me, I had not known,
Rose through my blood and every bone.

Arose I did like never before,
You brought me back, need I say more?

Helena Jaksic

SHOW ME

Show me a man
And I'll show you a smile
And if you possibly can
Help me through this for a while.

Show me who cares
And I'll show you who already does
Someone's got to be there
For me to feel their love.

Show me the path
And I'll show you my footsteps
Give me a head start
So that I have no regrets.

Show me that nothing has changed
And I'll show you what's to be
I won't let my feelings be rearranged
By you, him or anybody.

Show me what it's like
And I'll show you what it means
To have someone in my life
Instead of in my dreams.

Show me what I'd like to see
And I'll show you a full picture
To be close to someone is where I should be
For now and for the future.

Louise Allen

MONEY

Money, money, money, that's all people think about these days,
'You need money to survive,' Bob says.
Money buys clothes
Money buys stoves
And not forgetting special rings and other small things.
My mum's fighting, to earn us a living
But the more she earns, the more she is giving
However, money can't buy my mum's Christmas wishes
Or birthday kisses
And money can't buy seeing my dad's smile
When I have not seen him for a while.

Matthew Higgins (11)

I MEET MY YOUTH AT NIGHT-TIME

When I retire at 10pm, my age I know right well.
'Tis 50 years and adding, and that my aches do tell.
But something happens thru' the night, in my dreams, my grey is gone.
I return to when I was a youth, my age is 21.
There for hours I dance and play, I flirt and have such fun.
No need to have a rest time, where day is never done.
'Tis in the early morning, I have to leave my dreams.
Take a look into the mirror and wonder what it means.
For there's the grey haired old lady that somehow I seem to know.
'Tis then I find I am 56 and youth has had to go.
I'll see my youth again tonight, she knows not ache nor pain.
I look forward to my dream time where I can have fun again . . .

Rosie Hues

YOU DIDN'T ASK

You didn't ask to be conceived
You didn't ask to begin to breathe
You didn't ask to be mistreated
You didn't ask to be made to cry

You didn't have to face the future
You didn't have to live a lie
You didn't have to hurt yourself
You didn't even have to try

You didn't ask to fall in love
You didn't ask for the spark to burn dry
You didn't ask for the heart to flutter
You didn't ask to re-light the fire

You didn't ask to feel the pain
You didn't ask for personal gain
You didn't ask to shrivel and die
You didn't ask for the end of time.

Phil Clayton

ALL ABOUT YOU

My love for you will never die,
I just wanted you to know,
That I'm here until the end of time,
And I'll never stop loving you so.

This love is special,
A love only we could share,
And I'll spend my life with you,
Losing you I couldn't bear.

I'm so scared of losing you,
And I wish I could stop this blinding beam,
Because I'll lose you if I don't find the switch,
So let me wake up from this dream.

This love is special,
From the second I set eyes on you,
You gave me wings to fly,
And I want to spend my life with you,
Because I'll love you 'til I die.

Dave Stylianou

HEAVEN'S PARADISE

Heaven's glass door,
Heaven's golden chair,
Concealed in faith,
That champion light.

A book of stars unfold,
As an angel sits patiently,
Within her golden aura,
Lamenting of the Earth.

With man's indulgence,
The forest laid bare,
Within Heaven's paradise,
Nature is supremely evident.

Where colossal stars rotate,
Giving one endearing enchantment,
Maximising great interest,
With precision and enlightenment.

Spiritual and e'erlasting,
God is gracious and holy,
In spectacular fashion,
With abundance, wisdom and truth.

Immortalised for e'ermore,
Paramount and universal,
Spell-bound with respectability,
With purpose and charity,

With forgiveness and faith,
With commitment and clarity,
God is supreme and wondrous,
In a complex world that is unlimited.

Universal beauty, ordained gloriously,
Underneath the great canopy of Heaven.

James S Cameron

PIRATES

In the legends of pirates
They killed all scurvy scum
And plundered on the oceans
All for the glory of fun.
Legends say they had wooden legs
And a hook or two
A parrot on the shoulder
And a scarred and bloodied crew.
They stole and buried treasure
And then made a treasure map
They hoisted the Jolly Roger
Putting sailors in a flap.
They made their captives walk the plank
With a swash-buckling applaud
This was the mark of a pirate
Who knew the pirate code.

Donna Salisbury

LOVE OF A PC

Each day at seven I turn it on
Press its buttons and I am gone
I'm under its spell, hooked on its hum
Sitting in front of it on my fat bum.

I wiggle the track ball, tickle the keys
Hear its fan, feel its cool breeze
In love I am with the flat thin screen
A sight such as this has never been seen.

I draw silly doodles with my tablet and pen
Then play Scrabble, biggest score ten,
I might write an email or surf the net
It's quite amazing, the pleasure I get.

My scanner and printer go on at the end,
Their hums and clicks like the voice of a friend,
Make me feel good, happy and glad,
My computer, my baby, have I got it bad?

Joan Thornton

THE MOTORBIKE

It's out in the garage on its stand,
Where it sits, nobody stands.
It's red, black and chrome,
It will never have a better home.

Nor better love, nor better care,
It's like a king just sitting there,
It's taken out when there is no rain,
And if there is, it's brought back again.

It's dried, polished, put back on its stand,
You can look, go past, don't touch, understand.
But I think it's finally losing its place,
I'll not say anything, just in case.

But I wonder what will take its place,
Maybe another one taking up more space.
But between you and me, I really hope not,
For I think motorbikes are a real death trap.

Ina Higginson

REFLECTIONS ON GROWING OLD

We look back as we grow old,
The weather now, we feel the cold.
Summer we welcome the sun,
We enjoy ourselves and have some fun!

Travelled abroad and at home,
Enjoyed Italy and also Rome,
In the Navy, visited Aussie land,
Enjoyed it too, thought it grand!

Bill Drew

OLD BUT YOUNG

A senior citizen am I,
Young at heart, I prefer to be,
Pretty as a picture is what I see,
But my age doesn't agree
My body wants to go,
But the other half says no,
Dancing is so much fun,
But now I feel like a nun,
Love can be for all,
But companionship is all I recall,
My memories keep me young,
But that's about all.

Iris M Oldham

THE FUTURE

The future looks insane
All night, shouts
And cries.
Sirens, cars going up
And down.
This one way street.
Next door opens
Her door.
'Is this 1958
Or 2008?' she cries.

I close the door
And draw the curtains
Dazed by the blackness
Of it all.
Voices quoting
Marx
Stalin,
Mao.
Shouting,
'The city of the future of
Events, not yet taken place,
Is coming.'
Better to pile matches, bread
Candles from yesterday.
Crates of oranges
And potatoes,
Paper bags and tea.

Drinking alone in Paris
Walking with the dead
Internalised eyes.
Singles all around
Outlives the need for
Solitude, in these fraught,
Crowded times.

No witness to our life
Selecting things to buy
In this cul-de-sac, with
Activities and smells.
But for the moment, there's
No movement.
Nothing in or out
Showering in the darkness,
These mortals who will
Leave it too late.

Hello spring!

Sylvia Whiteford

FEELINGS

It's no good feeling bitter.
It's no good feeling sad.
It's no good always longing
for the things we've never had.
Far better to be hopeful,
face life with a grin.
Open up your heart and mind
and let the goodness in.

I always try and do all of this.

Doreen Anne Smith

THE CLIPPER

Not for the squeamish, this,
Heaving decks and sails in the sky,
Rushing through rough waters and rain
The wind ever screaming by.

Mighty masts, creaking with strain
Taut ropes, like steel rods, holding tight
Great hull pushing through rolling waves
Like the moon passing clouds at night.

Deep down, great rudder steering way
Hard pressed, by the tidal flow
Great strain on the ropes and pulleys
Holding course, on the right way to go.

Hull full of tea, rice and cotton
Not sparing the load and the strain
Full bent on the one concentration
To be fastest clipper again.

J R Burr

COLOURS OF THE RAINBOW

(To Brian - from your sister Carol)

Now your caring days are over
And you've laid your wife to rest.
'You' need to get on with your life
So I'm setting you this test.

It's the colours of the rainbow
That you have to walk right through
To let things go, learn to live again.
Here's what we're going to do.

Red is the colour of all memories,
A badly broken heart.
Just lock away these memories
And make a brand new start.

Orange is to put your life in order.
To plan another 'life'.
I know it will be very hard
Without your lovely wife.

Yellow is to see the sun
In a lovely clear blue sky -
Sit upon a bank of memory
And watch a stream roll by.

Green was a holiday in Ireland
One that you both had planned.
You picnicked on a grassy bank
And held each other's hand.

Blue is a sea of memories -
A birthday you both shared.
It doesn't hurt to cry outside -
At least she'll know you cared.

Violet is a bouquet of happiness.
Look towards another day.
Through the colours of the rainbow
You find a pot of gold - they say.

Indigo is the last of all the colours.
There are things I'd like to say,
'Clear your heart and mind of sadness -
Look towards a brighter life from today.'

Carol Handley

IF ONLY

If we could see life's road ahead,
Would we mortals lighter tread?
In our hearts contentment find,
As our daily paths unwind,
Love and praise the Lord each day,
Keep faith with Him along the way!
Be more tolerant - understand,
Ignore what hate and greed demand.
Always to ourselves be true,
Our faults and failings see anew,
Oh! mortals any wiser be,
If such a gift be given thee.

J Teresa Simpson

REQUIEM

Saw you yesterday
But saw you were not alone
Sitting side by side
But you were not together
Seemed more warder than wife.

B Williams

JAM MAKING

Sweet, sticky, stirring,
While smiling, she remembers,
Generations past.

Louise Wheeler

HAIKU

Here they come, freckling
the sunset - grey pigeons fast
flying homeward skies.

Louise Mills

A HAIKU HIKE

(Matsu Basho (1644-94) was arguably the greatest of all Japanese poets and an expert exponent of Haiku)

'Along back roads to far towns'

A last poetic pilgrimage
took Matsu Basho
out of his hermitage
home nook at Edo

up through highlands
north of the town,
then right across Honshu;

next he went down
the long west coast, to
end arduous journey,
near fifteen-hundred miles,
logged in his diary
called *Oku-no-hosomichi.*

Matsu still smiles.

David Daymond

ELEMENTS

Sunflower beams down
On its bright little neighbour
The smiling daisy.

This, my son and heir.
Warmth from the sun, breath from air -
With rain, will sustain.

I have sown a seed
Flower rewards my senses
With bountiful bloom.

Valerie Spiers

HAIKU COLLECTION

I

Purple lavender
Releases sweet aroma
After soft showers

II

Tsunami speeds in
Born of undersea upheaval
Drowning total all

III

Red setting sunset
Frames island in silhouette
Upon glassy sea

IV

Soft water and wind
Wearing eternally eats
Hard mountains away.

Ron Deen

HAIKU COLLECTION

I
Darkness steals across
the lawn as a cat creeps up
on a butterfly.

II
My new baby's fist
clings on to my finger and
imprisons my heart.

III
The white page lies blank
awaiting my tardy muse
who fails to arrive.

Marion Porter

GENTLY

Wake me with your rays
Lifting brown earthy blanket
To catch the day's eye.

Fold me in your arms
As time forgets its duty
And sings songs of love.

Creation's power
Roaring down mountain sides to
Lie silent and stilled.

Shirley Johnson

ONLY A ROSE

One forgotten rose.
Its vibrant colour fading.
Summer says goodbye.

Gladys Baillie

HAIKU

He turns to face her
Frames *the* question - hesitates
Faint heart ne'er wins girl.

Paddy Jupp

HAIKU - SEASONS

The snow crisp and white
Envelops the countryside
So fresh clean and bright.

Birdsong fills the air
Blossoms burst forth with fragrance
A soft breeze out there.

The days are alive
Long hours of activity
A time for learning.

Colours flutter down
A rich carpet is laid
Completing the round.

Caroline C Hunter

A Few French Haiku

French summer
Summer is fizzing
Wine and juice-filled ripe red fruit -
Splashing ruby drops.

Grapevine
Back home, we'll think of
This vineyard on this hillside
As we taste this wine.

Hot Day
Makes me gasp, so cool
Is the turquoise pool, rippling
On a white hot day.

Quercy
Quercy Blanc landscape:
Hilltop limestone village floats
In a sunflower sea.

Pigeonnier
Dovecote palaces:
Pigeonniers - for French fowl
Of a flygone age.

Alice Boden

TITANIC - A HAIKU

It's unsinkable
So its designers maintained
But it sank too quick!

Rowena

A COLLECTION OF HAIKU POEMS

Strewn dark green seaweeds
Mix and mingle in jetsam
Midst tide line white froth

Pale wax-like lilies
Beneath cool floating green pads
Rainbow trout shelter

Honeyed rose fragrance
Still sultry midsummer air
Bees murmur content

Silver trail on path
Snail shell aside stone anvil
Thrush family fed

Seeds swept on calm wind
Anchor in humble crannies
Nature's perfect choice

Blissful paradise
Awesome untrammelled waves
Paradise stolen.

Doreen Roberts

HAIKU

I

Streaks of colour flash,
In brilliant reds, blue and green.
Fishing kingfisher eats.

II

Sun gently sinking
Behind hill, casts purple shadows.
Bids peaceful goodnight.

III

Blossom tree perfumed,
Humming bird hovers, long tongue
Nature's nectar sipping.

A R David Lewis

THE HAIKU

The chainsaw favours some.
Nature's loss lay discarded here,
Upon the forest floor.

From death, life returns.
A host of bluebells gathered,
To celebrate the spring.

Philip Warwick

UNTITLED

A Cunning old carp in a brook
one day got stuck on a hook,
the angler cried, 'Ha ha,'
the carp replied, 'Ta ta,'
and swam away down the brook.

Ray Burslem

WIND GAME

The wind is not content to rest today
He hurries geese upon their southward flight.
He pirouettes with some untold delight
and hints at secrets, only half in play.
Sometimes he murmurs low what he would say,
to tease the trees and give small birds a fright.
They huddle now, preparing for the night
with heads tucked into feathered disarray.
But with the dawn they know without a doubt,
the secret that the wind held with such glee.
The muffled lanes and ermined branches show
what sent him into such an ecstasy.
He takes command with a triumphant shout
to tower drifts of freshly fallen snow.

Lois Leister

ELEMENTARY

Here it comes again
grey sky growls at helpless sea
spitting misty rain.
Like an artist's colourwash
blurring edges, triumphant.

Linda Bond

IF YOU

If you go away
My life will never be the same.
Oh, so blue will be the day
If you go away.
I'm walking on my way
Whispering your name.
Please, don't go away
Stay for me the same.

Dorothy Naboko

NICKI

There once was a girl named Nicki
Who seemed to love giving hickeys.
She kissed all the boys
With venomous noise,
Her lips to their necks were quite sticky.

D E Evans

LIMERICK COLLECTION

Simple Ann

'You should reduce the price of this armchair, dear Dan
It felt like I was sitting on a frying pan.'
'I should want some proof
To say that's the truth.'
'Here's the pan I used,' said Ann!

The Artful Banana Seller

'My bananas cost,' said Mister Lee,
'Fifty pounds each, with two for free,
So for each one you buy,
You save, I do cry,
A huge one hundred pounds, Miss Dee!'

The Strange Name

A crazy young girl by the name of Fay Fay
Said, 'What a strange name I've got, dear Ray.'
She sounds sane now, thought he,
Till she added, 'You see,
My surname's a bit odd too, I say!'

Joan M Wylde

In No Doubt

We are, who we are,
We cannot change that fact,
We do what we think best,
Have no time to act.

We are, who we are,
Though it's not always true,
Sometimes we pretend
Living lies with you.

We are, who we are,
Hate or love is just a feelin',
Forgetting when we can
Looking at the ceilin'.

We are, who we are,
No one person is to blame,
Turning back the pages
Things look the same.

We are, who we are,
Even in times of self-doubt,
Kicking up a dust storm
From the inside out.

We are, who we are,
We had no choice whatsoever,
Clown or Prince Charming
Yesterday, now or never.

We are, who we are,
We are born, we live, we die,
In truth we are ourselves
Until life passes us by.

George S Johnstone

LET THE POPPIES GROW

The poppies grow,
The poppies grow,
Hide the truth from them who know,
The simple pleasure of a smile,
Even if it takes a while.
Blood and toil the whole world saw,
Simple lands they're fighting for,
But nobody can even see
The scars they've left for our countries,
And the whole world doesn't know
How our faith has sunk so low.
Because we've got to become
This world's next generation,
What an example our ancestors set,
And pretty soon their ways we'll have met.
Now we've got to understand,
To take each other by the hand,
And let the peace grow naturally,
So the whole world can be free.
So now everyone will know
That we've let the poppies grow.

Jade Rigby (10)

DO DREAMS COME TRUE?

Have you ever had a dream come true?
Have you ever caught the moon?
When you go to sleep
Do you believe dreams are to keep?
Wrap them up in a sack
Pray that it's not too much to ask
For them all to come true
So you're not so blue.
Have you ever had a dream come true?
Will this world ever let you do?
I'll never give up on you
It's not what I do
I'll always cherish you
As I love you true
You're my dream, you see
Will you be mine to keep?
Will you be there when I go to sleep?
So I wake with you
And see a dream come true.

Matthew Holloway

THE IVY-CLAD COTTAGE

For sale! shouts the wee notice.
For sale, green windows, latticed
Wink their plea - oh won't you buy?
The poison ivy creeps so high
And its vice grip chokes too tight.
For sale - do please come and buy
And rescue me from my plight.

With my white walls not so white
And poison ivy now my blight,
Pretty was the verdant lace
With which once I hid my face.
My master was that dear, dear Lance
Whose broad grin did match his pace
Of lofty pride and beaming glance.

My green door hangs off its hinge
And the sole rose gone long since -
That used to stand by my door
To welcome all, both rich and poor.
And oh, that sweet delightful day
When Lance, all tired and so foot-sore
Brought home his lady Sally May.

The years have gone - they never last,
And the gay children's mirth has passed.
And my master, my dear Lance
Him of sated, lofty prance,
With sweet lady Sally May,
Has travelled to a world from hence
And gone forever and a day.

Thus I'm for sale - a sad, sad plight
Alone, forlorn and quite a sight.

While greater gales and storms yet blast
Strong do I stand, built to last:
Though ruined, in green mouldy veil,
Nothing of my glorious past:
Still do buy me - I'm for sale.

Liz Barnor

THE OSCARS

I just want to set the scene,
The crowds are out in droves,
The stars arrive in limousines,
All dressed in fancy clothes.
Red carpets laid out on the ground,
Photographers' cameras flash,
Security guards are all around,
At the film awards' great bash.
Fans, with pen and book in hand,
Seek autographs with zeal,
The stars sign with their magic hands,
It gives the fans a thrill.
Into the theatre the stars all go,
The places have been set,
It is one big, glittering show,
Just as you'd expect.
Great names are gathered here tonight,
Some old, and many new.
All are in the spotlight,
But Oscars for the few.
American stars, and British too,
Are hoping for their dream
To win an Oscar, one would do
To prove they've made the scene.
The nominations are now read out,
They sit with bated breath.
The stars who win, there is no doubt,
Will give their greatest performance yet.

B Page

A Day In The Life Of A Hospital Patient

The breakfast cart comes clattering in,
Filled with 'delights', which belong in a bin!
Tea or coffee in a plastic cup,
Weak and lukewarm, you need to drink it up.

Is that the time, it's nearly eight
And I've still got 27 pills to take!
'Take them all at once,' a nurse suggests,
They'll probably take all day to digest!

The newspaper trolley arrives on the ward,
Just as the doctors walk through the doors,
Wearing hipster jeans and belly button rings,
When did doctors become such young, trendy things?

Suddenly you hear your name being called,
And you're off to X-ray, just down the hall.
Out of X-ray in five minutes flat,
Then a two-hour wait, until someone can take you back!

2pm and your visitors arrive,
And ask how you have been, you answer, 'Just fine.'
'Where were you cut, and can we see?
How many stitches?' they ask gleefully.

'We're off now,' your visitors say,
And promise to visit another day.
Peace and quiet now, you finally think,
Oh no! It's time for another warm drink.

Not long until hot chocolate is served,
And definitely the best thing in hospital I've heard.
Snuggling down to try to sleep,
Something is flickering so you take a peek,
The main ward light is in need of repair,
The end of a restful day in hospital care!

Gail McPherson

My Road

I'm walking down your road,
But you weren't there,
Looking where to go,
Looking in despair.

All the thoughts in my head,
Are filled of you and me,
Past, present and how it could've been.

Finally I see your face,
I want to turn and run,
I don't know what to say,
To counter what I've done.

You turn your face away
To hide the hurt and pain,
I say it's not your fault,
And I'm the one to blame.

You're walking down my road,
Glance up for one last stare,
You know my world is over,
But you don't seem to care.

Sophie Collier (15)

A Salute

Here's to those, who fought and did fall,
Here's to those, who came to the call,
Here's to those, who perished in the cold,
Here's to those, whose truths will never be told

Here's to those, who sent them on a lie
Here's to those, who gave false reasons why
Here's to those, pockets filled with our gold
Here's to those, whose truths will not be told

Here's to the mother, whose love has died
Here's to the mother, her tears have never dried
Here's to the mother, in the shadow of cold
Here's to the mother, whose truth will be told

Jeff William Milburn

I PRAY THAT WE WILL

The unanswered question of 'Why?'
The unwanted tears that people cry
The senseless loss of God's creation
taken away by his very own people

What is the meaning of all this pain?
Why no sun but plenty of rain?
Power of the people and their bitter conflictions
as we get closer to Armageddon

The decisions of few lead the masses to suffer
The loss of faith in our very own Mother
The desire to terminate our own existence
What good can ever come of this?

I question what's right and what's wrong
I question what's short and what's long
I ask how can we possibly know when we are force-fed
and not encouraged to learn?

I stood at the spot where thousands once died
I stood there, I thought and I tried
to imagine their horror as the buildings came down
but the sheer thought of it made me dizzy

I remained silent as I read their names
I feel like a prisoner locked in chains
I'm confused by the enormity of it all
I'm grieving and I didn't even know you

I recognise your working lifestyle
I imagine you walking the Green Mile
You couldn't possibly have known what was going to happen
I wonder if this is a blessing

I sometimes feel so insignificant and small
I sometimes feel like I know it all
At times I feel like God herself
but my secretary misplaced the agenda

Where is it that we go from here?
Do my prayers fall upon listening ears?
Does anyone know if we will survive?
I pray that we will

Susan Macdougal

NIGHTLY SERENADE

Discordant callings in the night,
The jungle echoes the bantering cries,
Each voice claiming their moral right,
As through the trees, the soft wind sighs.

The challenging song of a night bird call,
The throaty rumble of animals near,
Each marking their patch, both big and small,
No sign of man to cause them fear.

Yet amongst this display of challenging cries
Respect is rife, as each nobly give
The masters their place, in their animal ways
They could teach us mortals how to live.

Spontaneous mirth they too can share,
This boisterous front, oft times a show,
Rapture, evident in the nightly air,
Where no human treads the earth below.

As a hazy dawn creates a crimson glow,
The nightly serenade soon fades away,
Silently, the creatures each prepare to go
And face the tumult of a brand new day.

Isaac Smith

THE SEASON

The wind is gently swaying the corn
Which grows taller since it was born
And in another field, there grows some hay
Which also stands tall to greet the day
Then going down towards the river's edge
There stretches alongside, a flowering hedge
Summer's nature is becoming of age
The circle of life's book, we turn another page
Chapter after chapter you read on and tend
To carry on because you are not at the end
When at last the book is finished and is put away
Then someone else finds, like the sun rays
Life begins again at the start of the circle of the year
To our lives, we hold very dear
So when we become old and begin to wither
No point in holding back and starting to dither
Like nature we are born to grow and die
So when we go, don't say goodbye
For we will be born again in life anew
Like the day that begins with skies so blue
And don't forget those that you know and love
They will never be below or above
You are surrounded with memories of their life with you
To life's mysteries you need no clue
You know there is nothing to attend
Because life never really comes to an end.

Anthony Jones

APPLEBY

Appleby-in-Westmorland -
It's really quite unique.
Always bright and friendly -
It's rarely cold or bleak.

It's in the heart of Cumbria,
Along the Eden Valley.
The river's really beautiful,
It makes you want to dally!

The trees are green and plentiful,
The willows gently sway.
The banks are full of flowers, wild,
So colourful and gay.

Hills and mountains all around,
Magnificent is the view.
Climbers come from counties wide
To see what they can do.

The sky is filled with countless stars,
The moon is shining bright,
A gentle breeze sways in the trees -
It is a lovely night!

Joan Packwood

A FRIEND

Sometimes in life we are blessed,
To have a friend who stands the test
Of all life's troubles, big and small
And by your side will face them all.
When days are dark and nights are long
Their love and loyalty so strong,
Even in the depths of deep despair
Support and comfort always there.

As dark clouds flood into your mind
When self-belief you cannot find,
A hand, a word, a gentle touch,
Will mean to you so very much.
This friend, that throughout all the years
Has shared your happiness and tears,
A neighbour, brother, sister, wife,
They bring such pleasure to your life.

So think of them, as they of you
And do return their friendship true,
As wealth can never feelings buy
No matter then, how much you try.
Life's path, though it be short or long
Decisions made both right and wrong,
One truth remains until the end
The greatest gift you have - a friend.

I A Morrison

DIET

I started out by loving you
then grew quickly to despise you.
You with your patronising ways.
You take advantage of my weakness,
waving another chocolate bar under by nose.
I give in . . . give it here . . .
bloody diets!

Pam McCormack

DRUG DEATH

I have a short tale to tell,
you should all know it quite well.
Here it is . . .
pain is harsh. Love is fast,
so let's shoot up and all go to Hell.
. . . To Hell with that!

Alana More

SANITY

It seems that sanity has died
Looking around, insanity survives
Will this world ever concede
To the rights and wrongs we all need
Somebody must update laws
For equality to be the cause
Of harmony within populations
And allow us peace throughout nations

BarbaraR Lockwood

An Inspirational Day In The Life Of The Wife Of The Poet

I open the curtains and gaze in delight,
At what I can only describe as a fabulous sight,
Mountains climbing high and very, very steep,
And the waters of the lake looking ominously deep.
Breakfast from the buffet, I choose whatever I will,
No inhibitions whatsoever, I just eat my fill.
No plans have been decided on how to spend the day,
Just select some venue, to there we'll wend our way.
The sun is shining warmly, there's not a cloud in the sky,
And so we pick out Mount Rigi, looking invitingly high.
First leg of the journey is taken by ship,
Second part on the mountain railway, a most scenic trip.
We alight from the carriage, almost at the top,
We climb a little higher, then gaze down at the drop.
Two sides are quite sheer, a third side is more graded,
So we descend down the latter, it's a little more shaded.
Half an hour's steady descent and a restaurant does appear,
A welcome relaxation with a glass of ice-cold beer.
Now on to the cable car and we swing way out into space,
It really is quite casual, there is no sort of race.
We arrive back in the village, and walk by the lake,
To our favourite little café for coffee and a cake.
Then it's back to the hotel for a bathe and a rest,
Soon be time for dinner, time to get dressed.
We enter the dining room, my favourite room of all,
Panelled walls and raftered ceiling, ideal for a ball.
Weggis is the village, Beau Rivage is our hotel,
By the side of Lake Lucerne, it really is quite swell.
I choose my meal most carefully, I select a bottle of wine,
This truly wonderful day really has been all mine.

George E Haycock

THE REAL SUMMER HAS BEGUN

The real summer has begun . . .
The skies were dark with ages . . .
I look upon my book and stunned,
Discover empty pages.

My wanderings would last awhile
To catch the waves that kiss . . .
So blue . . . and herring gulls so white . . .
They'd harmonise my peace.

The dragonflies would chase the light.
Have I had a dream?
Have I ever had a flight
With my broken wing?

The portion of my freedom waits
Lost between my days.
Have I ever got its taste,
Though granted anyway?

Eliza Kokanova

KENDAL CRASH, 1957

Imagine that September night when the news flashed
to the tenement yard on Sunlight Street,
that the excursion train had crashed.
When the man broke down and wept,
his sister torn from her seat as the song died in her mouth.
Imagine when the axle broke and the train ripped
into the tragic tenor of its journey south.

How the tree trunk gave way
to the wild burst; and how the door clanged
as the train ploughed into the yam field
near the sleeping town of Kendal.
The priest and pickpocket lending a hand
to someone else in its grip as the carriage
caved in and the hour sucked the oil from the lamp.

The instant when the train plunged
like a blunt machete through the damp clay
of a field flooded with moonlight, how the cows
broke into a dismayed gallop
when the metal shrieked and the cables took flight,
while rich and poor were thrust into the texts
of each other's lives, jam-packed, trying to hang on
between one world and the next.

Now year after year, as if to fill
some vacant post left by the chill,
the stories clamber back about the Kendal-ghost
emerging from the stricken stream
to hitchhike into town (or so they say)
then disappears, as in a dream,
like morning mist when it is time to pay.

Delores Gauntlett

AS ONE

We were as one in the beginning
Until life forced us apart.
Many grew the miles between us
Yet I kept you in my heart.
Through the changing of the seasons,
Through summer breeze and howling gale,
Our paths continued to meander
As we traversed hill and dale.
Sadly I've missed so many milestones
That have been scattered on your way,
Missed the sunshine and the shadows
That seem to make up every day.
My life has turned so many corners
Whilst broken hearts I've had a few
But no matter where I wander,
Every road leads back to you.

Rosemary Thomson

TEARY STAR

I only contemplated dreams of the night
To be one of those stars which shine bright
The reflection and thought of my eye . . . nothing but a star
Couldn't reach it though, because it was too far
So the exquisite star entered my eyes
Now with starry eyes I cry teardrops of light
Hitting the soil where the fallen lay, burning blades of grass
Struggling through the earth to reach at last
The dense and deep ocean where they passed
My glistening teardrops bringing light in the soil's darkness
Helping roses grow with an inevitable beauty
My dreams shattered like fallen glass
I believed this was the reason why quickly the days of the sun pass
The bitter cold approached silently but present full

My heart was the night, but my stars had fallen as tears
Dreams shattered the moon . . . so now the night, my heart,
possess darkness
Tell me what happens when your smile is empty?
Your frown shaken, your dreams shattered and blood-splattered
As my blood runs down in the most painful emotion
Similar to the bitter warm tears falling down a mother's angelic face
My soul was the earth and it's slowly slipping away?
What do you do when your soul can no longer pray?
My soul vaporising like mixed emotions of the Earth's sun and rain
However, the rainbow doesn't appear because there is no smile
The moon fights for its turn to shine as the sun backs down
The night once again rises victorious, but this time
My stars fall from my eyes, my moon is shattered to never be raised
From now there is only darkness . . .
No emotions, no love, no feeling, and please no praise . . .

Remembrance is not my worry . . . but to not know
that my brothers and sisters may or may not rise . . .
is my worry that lies in my heart.

Mohamed Abdullah Shariff

THE GIRL ON HORSEBACK

In the summer meadow,
I watch the girl on horseback -
She rides with innocence,
While from the river comes
A restful contentment -
The fresh ripple on the water,
Then a movement stirs my mind.
Quick again, the girl comes
Into the picture,
Riding through the heat haze.
I see one shimmer -
Of light, then speed and tranquillity
Come together -
Then the girl looks across at me.
She sees me from the opposite bank,
Stops, then canters on,
Between trot and gallop,
Till she rides out of view
Of studied observation.

Roger Thornton

CLEVER HANNAH MARIE!

Nana bought Hannah at four
A Christmas toy, a piano
Six years on, 28th March 2004
With girls and boys
Playing in Liverpool Philharmonic Hall
Not the piano, but her clarinet,
She stood ever so tall to give her all
Everyone proud, lovely sounds not too loud
For there were many at the Philharmonic
If music be the sound of life
Play on, play on, it felt right
What does Nana have to say
About 28th March, concert day?
I enjoyed as others tremendously
My spirit lifted, made me happy.
Well done, Hannah Marie,
Love being your nanny.

Rosemary Sheridan

AN ANGEL'S LULLABY

When angels are floating in
the midnight sky,
They're singing a lullaby to
babies on high,
They're gently swaying and
caressing them nigh,
They're rocking them soothingly
as they close their eyes,
Deep in slumber - in the midnight sky.

Jacqueline Ann Johnston

NICOLA

For a friend whom I hold so dear
Cold feelings beyond ice could not melt
Life had become my biggest fear
Death thought the cards had been dealt
So had I
But there was love
You
The selfish song I had been singing
Of self destruct and all being alone
Was broken through with the warmth you were bringing
Stops the turning of head and heart into stone
You
I
Not alone
Your kindness is so true
I write delicately placing you on a pedestal and throne
I am surely in debt to you
I say thank you
But two simple words could never be enough
With your selflessness and kindness you are more than most
                                        will ever be

My friend, how can I thank you
For being there for me?

Richard Marshall-Lanes

DAY TRIP TO BRIDLINGTON

The day we went to see the sea
We watched it crash upon the beach.
While the breeze blew through our hair
We used a telescope
To see how far the horizon could reach,
We watched seagulls
Hang on the wind and heard them screech.
The bobbing fishing boats
In the harbour gave us mal de mer.

The day we went to see the sea
We ate fish with chips by the ton.
And gorged on ice cream too big to lick
Everybody wrapped up
Because of the lack of sun,
And the only thing
That detracted from our fun.
Was the smell
From the fishing boats made us sick.

The day we went to see the sea
We played in the amusement arcade.
Grab a toy machine and penny drop
But as time passed
The amusement began to fade,
For our money
Got less the more we played.
I told the kids
That it was time to stop.

The day we went to see the sea
The kids argued all day long.
And inevitably it had to rain
The kids complained
About the constant seaside pong,
About the rain
And how the sun never shone.
But on the way home
They were asking to come again.

Keith Tissington

DOWN TOWN

One cold and windy night I went down town,
Never thought there'd be so many teenagers around.
Suddenly as a crowd passed by, I heard someone cry,
'What a bloody sight, he's wearing that tonight!'

Amongst the young men, not one jacket did I see,
But I noticed tears of cold, nestling in their eyes.
The ladies looked smart. Wore not a lot, it's true,
And I wondered if they knew their limbs were blue.

I was homeward bound, plenty of young uns swarming around.
Just then from across the way, a boisterous lass did say,
'Hey old biddy, you ought to be out of sight,
You don't dress like that down town at night.'

I thought, *Lassie one day you will grow old*
And who knows the day may come when you're told,
'Missus the way you're dressed sure is a funny sight,
Fancy wearing a coat down town on a Saturday night.'

J Booth

SLEEP LITTLE BABE, SLEEP ON

Sleep, sleep, little babe, sleep on
Lying on a bed of straw.
Who knows what the morrow will bring -
Shepherds will visit, angels sing
As they magnify the newborn King.

Oxen stood over His crib
Eager to take first peep
At the maker of Heaven and Earth
Lying asleep after His birth.
Sleep, sleep, little babe, sleep on.

Soon the morn will come
Over the snows will shine the sun,
And, at the breaking of the dawn
Will come the shepherds from afar
Guided by the first twinkling star,
So, while darkness covers the sky,
Nestling amongst the sweet, dry straw,
Sleep, sleep, little babe, sleep on.

Blanche C Rice

ODE TO THE BRIEF HISTORY OF TIME

To define an interval of time,
Take a comparison, make it rhyme.
Spin a world physically profound,
Like a celestial merry-go-round.

To companion the world's ethereal sprite
Take a sun, glowing crimson-red, bright.
There was dark, then came light.

Consider the transposition,
A contrasting disposition,
Empirical in its definition,
From an enigma to the sublime.

Now the interval in-between,
Is an intangible unseen.
To keep the metre and rhyme,
Give it a name, call it time.

Observe this gyration
By measuring the rotation,
And the reckoning will portray,
Twenty-four hours make a day.

The answer to this question
May be found in a suggestion
To take a look in a book
By a professor 'Stephen Hawking'.

Although you may find it daunting,
In the interpretation
There is an explanation,
Of this period of respite.

Between a day and a night,
An edition quite erudite.
To keep the metre and rhyme
A nomenclature to define.

Say, just for supposition,
Think of a title, give it a line.
You may then call it
'An ode to the brief history of time'!

Robert Reddy

My Ideal World

In my ideal world we'd all be equal
And would live for a hundred years
During that time the sun would shine
There would be no such thing as tears
No mental problems, sickness or disabled
Everyone healthy, fit and able
No one born deaf, dumb or blind
And the whole of my world would have to be kind
We wouldn't have terrorists, wars or disaster
Instead we'd have love with lots of laughter
We would all be happy, giving plenty of hugs
All alcohol-free and definitely no drugs
Our houses would be the exact same size
Where each family could enjoy their lives
No one would ever experience pain
There would be no storms, just occasional rain
Our children would have to make their own fun
As I'd never allow things like a BB gun
In my ideal world there would be no rules
No paid jobs, religions or schools
We would have possessions but we'd all have the same
We wouldn't need money as there'd be nothing to gain
In my ideal world, this would all be true
But I don't live there, and neither do you . . .

Dawn McClarren

WALKING ALONE

Walking alone at dead of night
Getting drenched in the pouring rain
Trying to hide from the street light.

Angry words explode in my brain
It's quiet, no sound from busy feet,
Will I have the chance to explain?

I see a policeman on his beat
Exhausted, I give a deep sigh
He walks with me along the street.

A moment's pause to say goodbye
Then I'm free to consider my plight
I'm startled by a barn owl's cry.

I return home to put things right
Walking alone at dead of night.

Rosemary Davies

BESLAN SCHOOL NUMBER ONE

The criss cross of the tangled struts now standing guard over
                                     Beslan's grief
Will haunt this world for evermore, with tales of horror and disbelief.
As the innocent were put to death, the fires of Hell burned into my heart
But still I cannot contemplate what type of human being took part
As children ran in terror
Another bullet found its mark
As error after error
Unleashed scenes so cruel and stark.

Charred and mangled girders of steel, that now reach for Heaven
                                          without hope
Will signify the souls we lost, but do nothing to help parents cope.
As the bodies burn within the heat of the Devil's latest victory,
Men of power try to justify why they seek to destroy liberty.
As sunken eyes glaze over
Another madman wields a knife
A child will lose its mother
And a husband has lost his wife

The vitriol will speak its hate, as the weak will be pawns in the game
Companions will become irate, but the dead child will not talk again.
As the images haunt my mind, I see naked shells reach out in fear
For the safety they could not find and the coffins and funereal bier
As families are torn apart,
The world looks on, then turns away,
They never did hear the heart
That stopped beating yesterday.

Vernon Norman Wood

THE VISIT

When Father Christmas came to London, he thought he'd have a fling
He said, 'I'll wear my bright red suit - I'm sure it's just the thing!'
Then he harnessed up the reindeer and flew off into the air
And it wasn't very long before he came down in Leicester Square
He kept ho, ho, ho-ing when he saw the 'ladies' ply their trade
And when one cuddled up to him, he thought his day was made!
When she whispered, 'Oh Father Christmas, please come round
                                                to my pad,'
The old boy quickly chuckled, 'Well! Well! That can't be bad!'
He had trouble with his buttons cos Mrs Christmas knew him well
And when he checked his reindeer, he suspected they might tell
Sadly he told his lady-love, 'My dearest I must go.
For this season is my busy time as I'm sure you know.'
Then he hurried from that little room so full of warm delight
And with a grin he climbed aboard and flew off into the night.

Now you know if Father Christmas is late coming to your home
It is pretty certain that the naughty man is having 'fun' all of his own.

Sally-Anne Hardie

THE VAGRANT

There's little truth in the drinking man,
Lies flow when drinking the wine from Hell!
There is no day to the drinking man,
Nor heeds he the chiming bell!
No clock has face, no hands of time,
The dark, the shadows are his blind.
As he wanders on in lonely pain
Come the night
Come the day.

Each one, to him, the same.
He has no home, no plot of land
No maiden's kiss,
No outstretched hand.
If he should die in vagrant sleep,
His soul and spirit keep!
Who was this man of honest face
In gaiety and laughing mood?

Now sits a lonely soul
In chosen solitude!
Was he an actor?
Was he a king?
Was he a man
Who once had everything?

And when a coin is pressed in hand,
The giver walks in easy pace
To leave behind a lonely soul
To find a hiding place!
No war is won
If by dagger
Or the gun,
To stand up straight
Or stoop in gait!
Who is the better man?

Pamela Hanover

A MATRIARCHAL BEAUTY

In her aristocratic family; her likeness was so defining,
Her pleasant manners were often sincerely shining.
She had been widely viewed and admired by millions,
Aside, she was an icon who possessed her discretions.
The Duke of York, she was delighted to marry,
In the gist of her life, a new title arose for her to carry.
A royal designation had become ubiquitously unforeseen,
Her husband's rise to the throne had made her Queen.
Privately keeping her thoughts and feelings to herself;
Her comments on the abdication were placed on a shelf.
A notorious affair was disturbing her whole guided life,
Reluctantly taking the responsibilities of a ruler's wife
Public discretion had always been extensively laborious,
To many spectators, she's sustained a life quite glamorous,
Endured two world wars and incessant family scandals,
She glistened amidst a cantankerous chandelier of candles.
Courteously mute, she retained her dignity and refinement,
Impeccably elegant, she possessed unbounded sentiment.
Long-lasting, she was able to celebrate her centennial,
Her prominence as a great-grandmother was still congenial.
Outliving her husband, two princesses and never losing face,
Once her time was up, she had left the public eye with grace.
Her life was grand, as it ended under the light of the sun,
God above had granted her a lifespan of a hundred and one.
Her timeless smile and optimism were always utterly shown,
Within her short reign, she was able to stand on her own.
Always confirming goodness and her prevalent gratitude,
History will remember her tolerance of devastating vicissitudes.

Gracie-Jean Lovemark

ONE BY ONE, ONLY THE GOOD DIE YOUNG

Why did I have to die so young?
Why did I have to stop having fun?
At twenty-three my life's just begun.
Am I that bad?
Have I made people that mad?
Well now that I'm dead, I'm sure they'll be glad.
A forest of pain erupts in my heart
A sharp shooting pain in my chest like a dart
I didn't think it would be so lonely living apart.
But like a friend once said,
'There must be a lot of young in the dead.'

Chris Flett

TIME

Time scurries on as if I were not there,
Oblivious, it steals my life away,
And at the end of yet another day
I feel debased because it does not care.

Inanimate of course, and yet somehow
It oversees the passing of a man,
From birth to death records his earthly span,
Unmindful of the fickle here and now.

And thus our lives enact a wild goose chase
Unfolding deep inside and all around,
With head in Heaven, feet upon the ground,
Confounded by the realms of time and space.

We come, we stay awhile, and then we go,
To Father Time unwillingly a slave,
Our lives careering onwards to the grave,
As surely as the great seas ebb and flow.

The green leaves turn to brown, the brown leaves fold,
And scatter in the autumn wind and rain;
A lonely bird pipes out a brief refrain,
And I am feeling small and very old.

Time renders no ill humour, holds no grudge,
Retains no malice, causes no one harm,
Allays no fears, knows not rage nor calm,
And yet is both our jury and our judge.

Enchanted by a solitary bell,
Uncertain, should I laugh or should I cry
I ponder on my life as time rolls by,
Regretting little, wishing others well.

Brian Foster

BESLAN - FIRST DAY AT SCHOOL

I remember it - my first day at school
The smell of it, the new cut grass
The soap inside my cotton bag
From some old dress my mother made
The tang of polished wood from classroom floors
Or cabbage and potatoes waft down corridors.

The sight of it - the grey and crumbling
Walls of chiselled stone
So big for one so small to fit into
Or so I thought when I was four.
The touch of Mama's hand, now gone
The sound of my own breathing in my chest
These things I memorise within my mind
The day I started school.

I remember it - their first day at school.
A day as filled with hope as any other
When *they* had smelled the grass
And touched their mothers' hands or heard the bell
And tasted the sweet promise of success.

Until their dreams were sacrificed
Upon the altar of a stranger's cause
That shattered and destroyed
A thing as fragile as an angel's wing
And left our souls bereft.
But we can hold their missing futures in our hearts
To let those wings take flight and gently soar
Upon the softer winds of summer days
Or in-between the corners of our sleep.
These things we keep in memory for what they lost
The day they started school.

Lynda Tavakoli

JUST A DREAM

I never get to tell you
What I'd really like to say
How much I long to hold you
Each and every day.
To kiss you and caress you
And leave this world behind
There isn't any limit to the pictures in my mind.
You're the fuel of my fantasies
And the substance of my dreams,
In my special world it's you and me,
And nothing in-between.
But when I come back to Earth
And face reality, I realise . . .

It's just a dream . . .

Nargas Abdullah

UNJUSTIFIED

So now that your deed has been done,
An evil deed, cruel, 'Such a shame, so young,'
You have even begun to believe the story you've spun,
You're the only one, though; the fight for justice has just begun.

Millions of glares on your sick, guilty face,
As the jury opens an inevitably ending case,
Scared now, just like them, with no one to embrace,
Feeling horrid now, aren't you? Well, that's your place.

You spin your web of cold, calculating lies,
Your lawyer can't even defend you as hard as he tries,
You tell him the story about how they died,
It's unbelievable, merciless, and unjustified.

The verdict was predictable, guilty as charged,
Those involved, their problem shared, not yet halved.
Two life sentences, justice discharged.
You've still got the truth though, which from their families you've
wrongly starved.

It's not justice yet, just look at the facts,
Without you in the world two lives would be intact,
Think for a minute while you're rotting in your cell,
About what you've done, *murderer,* about the story you've yet to tell.

Amy Fullwood

THE JOURNEY

Gentle whispers touch my mind
Like softly wafting winds . . .
And in my heart - long suffering,
Awakening begins . . .
And lifts me from this mortal place
To fathom depths within,
Then pulls me from my reverie
To ponder life again.
What brings us to this holy place
And forces us to see
The blessings all around us . . .
And our yearning to be freed
From fears we find in loneliness,
That scatters dreams afar,
'Til not one trace can e'er be found
Not here - nor in the stars?
For you, my friend, are all I have,
And all I'll ever need,
Walk with me through the fire
As I walk along with Thee.
Then, side by side, we'll start the climb
To heights we've never known . . .
And when we reach our destiny,
We'll know that we are home.
Eternal, is the love you give
Forever is the peace . . .
And at the journey's end we'll find
The light has been released.

Deborah Gail Pearson

DOWN BY THE DUCK POND

Riverside Park is the name of the place,
You can stroll, cycle or jog,
With no traffic in your face,
But you meet the occasional dog.

It's really a picture of dreams,
Bridges here and there,
Built over small streams,
Even the train stops if you have a fare.

The wide path winds through well-kept grass,
Forty acres in all, I am told.
The penned-in dog run is class
And there's seats to rest if you are growing old.

Then there's the centre point,
Known as the duck pond.
Feed them, you must, touch them, you don't.
With them, some locals have grown a bond.

Let's not forget about the playground,
Full of swings and slides for the little ones.
If off they fall, there's not a sound,
Because the soft tiles save their young bones.

You can have a game of football with your hubby,
You can even have a round of golf.
Or maybe fishing is your hobby,
The Riverside Park is definitely a one-off.

Now if you feel like strolling further,
Down through the trees you can meander
Gathering raspberries as they grow,
Till no further you can go.

This is our treasured walk,
3.28 kilometres long, even in the dark
We must cherish the staff who work and don't talk.
Let's be ever grateful for our Riverside Park.

Beth McCracken

TRUE BEAUTY

From the creator, who's loving and wise.
Whose majesty shows in the sunrise,
With so many colours to choose.
How could you ever lose
The brilliance of His created Heaven and Earth?
Every day is like waking up to a new birth,
With the sun that appears, to keep you warm,
Still brings you light, even in a storm.

Diana Rowson

ISOLATED BY BURNS

My thoughts, my dreams, you are always there,
Eyes wide open but asleep in despair,
Constantly needing, probing away,
Eating away at my sanity, endorphins in disarray.
Why do you torture me, for innocence is mine?
Dark clouds have now gathered, there's no more sunshine,
For two became one, now one becomes a few,
All in my mind, shouting, spitting and crude,
I will clasp my hands together; look up to the heavens and pray
Please save me from my madness, please show me the way.

I exist in-between worlds of reality and fantasy,
The two are merging, clouding my judgement and sanity,
Your presents is forever with me, in my breath, soul and mind,
Tearing away at my heart, riding every beat that you find,
I want to be rid of you, I need you to leave,
I have served my sentence; I have done nothing but grieve,
This sadness seems endless, forever haunting my soul,
The harder I fight it, the harder the goal,
True love is forever, but s well as pleasure, it brings pain,
Killing me in silence, with my mind playing games.

Robert Cocking

SUSAN'S FIFTIETH BIRTHDAY SONNET

*(Dedicated to my sister-in-law on her fiftieth birthday, Mrs Susan Mooney and her
husband, Bill, my younger brother)*

The bluebird of paradise sings of love,
Celebrates Susan's fiftieth birthday,
Its loud, threshing song, harvests joy this day:
O Eden, valiantly, sail like a dove,
Bounteous wings, embroil a glove
Of rolling stars: surround Bill's way,
Love Susan eternally, never sway
From his gracious, good wife, held above
All other women, in his soul, heart, mind:
O', bluebird of paradise fly to Susan,
Sing loud this fiftieth year of life, find
Love in paradise, forever you can:
Bluebird of Heaven, sing very proud,
Susan's fiftieth birthday, love very loud.

Edmund Saint George Mooney

AUTOBIOGRAPHY

When urged to write account of life
I've spent, by friend who thinks there's tale
That's worth the telling, laughter's smiles
At once engulfed my thoughts. It seems
A glossy cover leads astray.
The pages they enclose are just
A catalogue of routine years.
I'll grant I've worked in places few
Have seen, apart from those for whom
It's home. I've done some things that few
Have done. I've been involved in rare
Events that seem like extracts torn
From novel's page. But none were planned.
To me it's more a case of storms,
Or days in sun, that came and went,
While I just carried on as though
Each day was normal gift. At times
I've had a close exchange with death,
But soon escaped to live again.
I've met a rich array of men
And women drawn from diverse walks
Of life, both high and low. With some
I've clashed. With most I've relished each
As I've beheld the child behind
The mask. The only tale I'll tell
Is one of thanks for love, for wife,
For children too, for their's as well.

Henry Disney

THE START OF OUR DAY

I rise early each morning, to walk my dogs
Into the woods we hurriedly trod.
It's so relaxing, there's no one around
Only the creatures that live in the woods to be found.
The peace and tranquillity starts off my day
It makes me set for anything that comes my way.

We make our way up to the top of the hill,
Into the field, were the scenery does thrill.
No one disturbs our silent thoughts
It's when I think things out and sort!
Only the noise from the trees
Singing gently as they sway in the breeze.
The view is stunning, it makes me feel good,
To live in a town with nature where I'm stood.

It's great to watch the wildlife at play,
When the rabbits see us they run away.
Squirrels running around the trees,
Chasing each other, it's a pleasure to see.
If you're lucky a deer you may spot
They are clever they watch, where you're off.
Then just a slight movement behind a tree
They know they have been spotted, they suddenly flee.

Now and again you get a real treat,
Quite a rare sight in the day if a badger you meet.
Often any time of day you will see the fox array
Little fox cubs chasing around, in the field they are usually found.

Woodpeckers drilling in the dead wood,
Insects fleeing from the birds that stood.
Our walk over, it's time for home,
We will leave the wildlife, free to roam.

Marilyn Pullan

FREEDOM FROM FEAR

The fear of pain I often find
Is worse to bear than any pain
Once the fear invades the mind
It grows, expands within the brain.

That ice-cold shaft of dread
Which in each thought appears
To hang high above your head
As an icicle of needless tears.

Through the dark and lonely nights
Those whose lives with faith are blessed
When faced with far of pain, do not take fright
But reach out to pray to Jesus for His healing rest.

Mercies new every morning He initiates
Bringing a strange new kind of peace
God works in power to disintegrate
That fear, that sword of Damocles.

Mary Spence

A VISITOR FOR TED

Ted! Open your eyes and look at me;
Don't fall asleep, or you won't see what I've brought today;
I think I ought to say that you'll probably be surprised.
Here it is, Ted!
It's an old and faded photograph of the two of us
which I've had enlarged for more clarity;
There's no disparity between us - just two soldiers, side by side.
Ted! Weren't we a good looking pair?
But sixty years ago we both had hair - and our own teeth
and hidden there beneath our uniforms, bodies, fit and strong.
How we've changed, Ted!
You, now in hospital bed, me in a wheelchair;
Though it must be said, that at least we survived,
and weren't suddenly deprived of life before it had begun.
Ted! How could we have known the cost?
That over 110,000 lives would be lost such a short time after
we two were photographed, awaiting orders to embark;
Destination Normandy, Ted!
6th June 1944 - now, sixty years later we're still hoping
that war will end one day;
Oh Ted, by the way, here's another photograph;
It's of my grandson - in Iraq!

Tony Reese

I'M EIGHTY-FOUR YOU KNOW

Hey Anna, you're sixty now they said,
lay down your tools, an extra hour in bed.
Put up your feet and have some tea,
enjoy a great long holiday.
They didn't understand you see,
God may not halt our ministry.
My prophetic gift, he did not withdraw,
and do you know, I'm eighty-four.

My widow friend, a word for you,
I really know what you've been through.
No man to feed, an empty bed,
and all the tears that you have shed.
But don't despair, there's things to do,
my God has not forgotten you.
On eagle's wings you too can soar,
come fly with me, I'm eighty-four.

To prove a point I'll have you see,
just what the Lord has done for me,
A special gift my God declares
as I resort to prolong prayers.
Through temple gate, a family came,
I felt compelled to ask their name.
A word then came to my innermost core,
yes, to an old lady, I'm eighty-four.

Oh praise God, what did I see
the one from all eternity.
Within His mother's arms He lay,
the Christ child of eternal day.
Salvation to the world He brings
this Lord of Lords and King of Kings.
So praise the Lord and pray some more
till you my friend, are eighty-four.

Albert Watson

A Rhyme For Our Time

Together two brothers make a handsome pair
Both dressed up with lots of hair.
Remember the mirror you could not pass
The comb came out to comb that black mass.
Always sleek and in its place
Not a hair on your face.
Now today it's a different story
Of the brothers who lost their crowning glory.
In those days they were young and slim
But nowadays they've lost their trim.
The years have passed, the looks have changed
As they have with others some parts have rearranged.
But never mind, to the folk you know
You'll always be Brian, we all love you so.

Jean Adam

THE ORANGE

They say, 'You can't do a rhyme with orange,'
Which to me seems rather strange.
If you can't do a rhyme with orange,
You'll just have to make it change.

I could make the end into range,
If I play around with the word.
But I'll lose the vital round O,
It won't be even heard.

If I lose the round O for orange,
It could become a square.
To play around with its segments,
Won't really seem quite fair.

I suppose it could be peeled
And given a different name.
Perhaps if I called it a mandarin
The rhyme wouldn't be the same.

Satsuma's a possibility,
It's still got the same a-peel,
But an orange is an orange,
That's just the way I feel.

You can't do a rhyme with orange,
No matter how long you spend.
I've tried to rhyme with orange,
But it's true, I think, in the end.

Dorothy Foster

THE PATH LESS TRAVELLED

An overgrown path, entwined with nature's trouble
A mass of lyrical perfection, baffled in spiritual muddle
A complex infrastructure of unknown culture
Visually original, invincible as the collective picture

An epic sanctum, lamented in stickiness
Crawling ignorance behind closed lids of an audience
Drowning the taste of nature's earthly bustle
Silky laughter like crystal-kissed descriptions

Blanker than whiteness; an expressionless dress
Hiding the synthetic skin of realness
Masking the translucent races and double faces
In the wild, suffocating depths of unconsciousness

Consistently persistent in the ignorance of insolence
Continuously transparent to the capacity of spirituality
Infinite minds caged in the security of logical certainty
Emotions fuelled with the energy of incomprehension

Paul Theoret

THE WORD YOU

Let us not make too much unnecessary fuss
Over the distance now trying to separate us
Actually amounts to nothing much
If you take into account that such
Strong feelings will connect
Us always, carefully dissect
The essence of our being in order
To contraband it over the border
The facetious frontier
Which is held so dear
By unbelievers
Whose fevers
Whose illness is in the mind
Renders them deaf and blind
To love
Above
Their barriers of misconception
We fly and we are no exception
In this
Bliss
Many multitudes are united
And though the short-sighted
Might triumph at having succeeded in separating
Their bodies, their hearts won't stop reverberating
With unsuppressed
Emotion possessed
By a kind of need
By the only creed
Of those other minds that instead are simple and true
A need that uncannily reminds me of the word you.

Giula Sandelewski

A NEW DAY

Every day is a new day,
A day to plant, a day to reap, a day to love,
A day to keep you away from harm,
To keep you ever in my arms.
A day when life is so good,
A day that makes me very glad
A day to keep you oh so close,
A day to love you the most.
A day to be happy, glad and free,
A day when wars will be no more,
A day when life will be a joy,
A day when pain will be forgotten
When God will be all we need,
A day when we will all take heed
And stop the fighting and the evil,
A day when we will jump for joy,
A day of laughter, girl and boy
When all the world will join their hands
A day when we will understand,
So let us show we really care
And pray that love is ever there.

Joyce Lawrence

MOON MADNESS (OR THE MOON AND I)
(After a visit to my husband who has Huntingdon's Disease)

I talked to the man in the moon last night,
I told him of our endless plight,
I said to him, 'I don't want to fight,'
I asked him, 'When will things turn out right?'
He never said a thing!

I only spoke the words in my head,
I mentioned some of the things we both said,
I said, 'I can't sleep at night in my bed
I get up feeling old and my eyes are red.'
He never said a thing!

I try to see things from every angle,
I think and think, while my brain seems to jangle,
I sort out my thoughts that are one big tangle,
I want to float in space, just hang there and dangle.
He never said a thing!

I may just go mad, to forget for a while,
I will just sit and rock in my 'rocker' and smile,
I may not talk any more, and just act senile,
I could try pulling faces, make folk run a mile.
He must be deaf! Poor thing!

Christine May Turner

BRIEFLY

They met briefly, their hands touched momentarily,
Then she left in a froth of satin and lace,
The memory of that transient moment
Dominated his thoughts; invaded his space.

She gazed from boardings twenty-feet tall,
Smiled enchantingly from magazine stalls,
He opened his paper and there she would be
Dressed for night-clubbing or a fancy soiree.

He might as well live in outer space,
She was way out of his reach,
Living in her sumptuous flat,
How could he compete?

That bitter-sweet meeting; so brief had caused him such pain,
He vowed that such a moment would never occur again.

Better by far to settle for something less
Than to get oneself into such an emotional mess.

Lil Bordessa

CRIME ON OUR STREET

There is a profit-making crime on our street
Extracting money from us, so discreet
The law ignores, as they sit and wait
Then they catch us in a trap, with no escape

One hundred pounds release, reads the notice so high
Instant cash, no credit, the price sky high
No excuses, no compassion, no regret
Just phone us, pay up to get out of the net

To get rich quick, I'll become a clamper
Making your wet, winter day, much damper
Two minutes late, or on private land, a ticket as you walk out of sight
But would my conscience let me sleep at night?

How can a clamper be so nasty, mean and tight?
How can a clamper sleep at night?
How can they trap us with no escape?
Trapping animals this way causes much outcry and debate.

The answer is, clamp the clampers while they're clamping
Then as he jumps from his van with angry feet stamping
You just smile, say no excuses, the release fee you will have to pay
While you were clamping me, you parked outside the parking bay.

John Edwards

I'M THINKING THAT

Now I'm in my sixties,
My image I should change,
My wardrobe, my make-up,
My hair I'll rearrange.

I'll wear bigger knickers,
That reach up to my chest,
And all year round
I'll wear my thermal vest.

I'll buy a flowery, flouncy frock
And a big, pink, floppy hat,
I'll fill my garden full of roses
And with passers-by I'll chat.

I'll pester the council
And make cakes for the church bazaar
And now I've got my bus pass
I could even sell my car.

I could go on half price day trips,
To take me here and there
And join the OAPs
For a demonstration in the square.

But on looking back I'm thinking,
That's not quite what I want to be
So I'll put it all on hold for now
Until I'm sixty-three.

C V Perkins

THE NINETY DEGREE ANGLE

An angular love found instead of round.
Its edges an agony of past, present and 'if only'.

Isosceles or acute, the angle's ever lonely.
Distances between then turning gravely, but abound.

Sharp wit, pointed favour, tight spots, the here and now.

Circumferences are missing, pregnancy dismissed boldly
And one finds all peace gone. Gnawing, lingering, longing.
The pyramid always entombed and in history was found.
Lascivious folly, placid joy or guileless mirth
Mirror melodrama, sadness or tragedy.

Perception and truth will not remain
Ever here on this middle-aged rock, this Earth.

While hieroglyphics reveal joy, not only malady,
The division and union are our love and pain.

Maria Katelaris

LIGHT

I see the night stars
And ask what is their meaning
That they light my way

Humans are like light
Particles and sometimes waves
Life needs self and love

Forever amber
Halted by the lights? Suggest
You get out and walk

Light's baby brother
Is the darkness of twilight
Or dawn's sweet promise

Walk into the light
Seek to own your self's shadow
Arrange your own space

Margaret Chisman

RESOLUTION

How I wish I woke up in the morning
Instead of halfway through the night,
Oh the joy it must be when day dawning
To rise with the lark at first light.

To my shame when the sunlight comes spawning
A new day of hope and delight,
I'm adorning that place I was born in,
Disgraceful you say, and you're right.

I can think of but one sound solution
To ease this somniferous blight,
I will make a new year's resolution
To arise all merry and bright.

I can start with a chilly ablution
Then partake of a trifling bite,
Wash it down with a caffeine dilution
Then go give the milkman a fright.

Yes, that's what I'll do, I'll do it, don't fear.
Yes, that's what I'll do, next year.

R K Bowhill

DISTANT HILLS

On the clearest of days
I can see distant hills.
Snow blessed hills,
English hills.
Dove breast, grey scree
outlining flamingo snow fields
as the March afternoon sun
emblazons the high horizon

And any day
I can see Criffel

But these are not the clearest of days.
All around me I can see
the ash grey smoke of death
driven by the wind,
clinging to God forsaken fields.
The chilling, killing fields,
as the louring March dusk reveals
empyreuma of heartless hellfire.

Yet even today
I can see Criffel.

Gerry Robertson

MY FAVOURITE COLLEEN AT THE DANCE HALL

Mary was a colleen of unbounded beauty, so rare.
With red, curly hair sweeping down on her shoulders in the air.
She wore a very short, orange dress with spots of green.
So her pretty legs could be clearly seen.
I asked her kindly for a dance, please
We orbed together on the floor, softer than leaves
Our supple bodies moved with such ease.
Round and round went, our necks
With alluring power of the Irish jigs dancing contest
No other couple dare to wreck!
Finally, we won, happily from rest
We snatch one or two departing, loving kisses
As we had a magical night of exciting dancing bliss!

Sammy Michael Davis

ASHES

We sat talking by the fire
thinking each our heart's desire.
She told my fortune, from the coals,
I'd be rich and drive a Rolls.
But it seems she read amiss
and instead of life-long bliss
I've been wondering where the cash is,
and the coals are long-since ashes.

Frank J Mills

JOIE'S SECRET

I fall asleep, laying in my bed,
I hear a laugh, a child-like giggle,
I awaken startled,
I search my room to find nothing,
I hear footsteps outside my door,
I'm drawn towards it,
My door creaks open before my hand can reach it,
Nothing.
I hear the laugh again and footsteps,
I follow the eerie sound,
I catch a glimpse of a little girl with black hair,
She's wearing a white dress and small black shoes.
I follow her,
I hear a scream,
I run into the room,
The little girl is lying on the floor,
Her white dress stained red,
Stained with her own blood,
Secrets never die until they are told,
I tell the story of her death for her
And lay her down to rest.

Scott Ottaway

THE PAWNS OF NATURE

Squared dimensions of measured time,
Borderline chess mapped of divisional continents,
White is the foamy sea, black represents islands and countries,
Daylight shines from the pieces of white,
Darkness contrasts the silhouettes of black,
Movement of the blazing sun from dawn to dusk,
The dancing of the moon lights the level land.
Government Kings of order and command,
A Queen of states in a variation of moves,
To do as she pleases is to no one's surprise.
Castles of powerful armies to control,
Manoeuvring politicians, brave are the Knights to evade,
World nations are Bishops swift to embark in fullest of flight.
Pawns of the living stand on the front line,
The day and night, ordinary people,
Tectonic plates engaged and encounter,
Mother Nature shakes the wind of a violent storm,
Tidal fury consumes and engulfs,
Human puppets are helpless in their plight,
Fragile pawns are tossed and thrown,
Breaking bones of tangled flesh,
All are pulp in wooden mash.
Homes, shops, temples and towns,
Tropical stress on swept away beaches,
Matchstick boats torn to pieces,
All are lost in a shadow of madness.
Pick up the broken and the dead,
Throw them all in graveside boxes,
Where children played, families lived, villages stood,

A barbaric mud pit of Hell is all that is left.
Bloodstained memories lie in a mass burial site,
Survivors must climb the mountain of broken dreams,
Then bury the empty faces that stare in the mirror of life.

Nigel Astell

AS EACH MEMBER DOES ITS PART

As each member does its part - 'O' don't be daft,'
Said the finger to the scapular and laughed.
'I'm working every day without a penny for my pay
So I'm giving up the job this very day.'

'I don't blame him,' said the kidney to the toe
'This work is full of misery and woe.
Cleaning blood every day without a penny for my pay
How can anyone expect me to stay?'

So the mutiny went on throughout the body
Instead of work, many took themselves a hobby.
A few old faithfuls they did stay, carried on from day to day
But the body did not function as it may.

Now the outcome of the strike was not so good
Because the body didn't function as it should.
So discussions were begun on how the system should be run
But it was much too late, the deed was done.

Rigor mortis had set in, I'm sure you'll know
Though the body looked so peaceful there on show.
All the signs of life were gone, the race had all been run
And the living of that life had all been done.

Now the moral of this tale, so well we know
Is that the body of Christ down here below
Consists of you and me being what we're meant to be
To keep the body working in perfect harmony.

Daphne Kynaston

UNFINISHED SONNET 4

Shall I compare thee to thy hero Arthur?
Thou art more exceptional and farther.
If I am Guinevere, thou shalt be to,
For she true loved Sir Lancelot.

Oh, love! Dear love, just to be near thee,
'Tis most simply stated, sweet ecstasy.
What silver words from silver tongues do slip
And lovely fall over versed lip?

Mine own fairish words cannot justly show
They most ironic beauty known.
Philosopher knight of constancy,
'Tis classic virtue that propels me.

Emerson Richards

As I Walk

As I walk all alone
Through this world
Of loneliness, sadness and sorrow,
I think all the time of two angels
From up in Heaven above
Two very beautiful angels
Who I will always love
With the whole of my heart and soul
For those two beautiful angels
Are the ladies in my life
One is my beautiful, five-year-old daughter
The other is my tender, loving wife
And those two beautiful ladies
Fill my happy heart
Full of warm, tender love
And my very lucky life
Full of joy and happiness
And the names of those two
Beautiful angels
Are Linda and Marie.

Donald Tye

GRUMPY OLD WOMAN

The decorations have gone, thank goodness say I
Christmas is over, I think with a sigh.
No good mornings, Happy Christmas to you,
From people who don't want to know all the year through.
The turkey's all gone, the mince pies too,
I've put pounds on, more than a few.
Unwanted gifts have gone into a drawer,
They'll do for presents next Christmas, if not before.
My money's all gone, oh what a bore,
Can't go out for a month or more.
'Happy New Year,' now neighbours say,
Same to you, it's flipping cold today.
The gas bills come in, the electric one's due,
The council tax and house insurance too,
The telephone bill has grown quite a bit,
Grandaughter's got a mobile which proved quite a hit.
The sales started last spring and haven't stopped yet,
Folk are spending money they haven't paid back yet.
Is this really what Christmas is all about
Sometimes I want to stand up and shout,
'Remember it's Christ's birthday, God's gift to us.'
A grumpy old woman, maybe that's what I've become,
So I'm cancelling Christmas and New Year chum,
I'll sing some carols in the church up the road
And thank God for His Son and for bearing this heavy load.

A C Iverson

THE LONELY CHILD

Do you really want to know how I feel?
Do you really want me to express and reveal?
All that I can let on is that I am feeling very sad,
I sit and cry myself to sleep some nights,
so you can imagine it's pretty bad.
Thoughts and fears have a hold over me,
spiralling out of control, unable to break free.

Do you really know what scares me so much?
Do you really know how I dream of someone to touch?
I never experienced the love of a male figure during my early years
people who were once so close to me
didn't always appear how I thought they'd be.

Do you really understand the many thoughts inside my mind?
Do you really understand that I'm not quite sure
what I'm looking to find?
It feels as though I'm trapped in a maze
pondering with worry, trying to engage.

Do you really see the truth when you look into my eyes?
Do you really see the truth because I'm very surprised?
For I have as good as lied to you about who
I am inside
but to be honest
I know not what is going on with me,
because I am just as blind.

Frances Morrison

THE OLD ROCKING CHAIR

I still see it there, the old rocking chair
with Granny sitting in the corner.
The fire aglow, kettle always on the boil.
Deary me, let's have a cup of tay.
Griddle with the tattie bread, home-made soup
with a spud or two, country salted butter,
home-made jam, soda loaves on the bake.
Granny with her hair tied up in a bun,
her snow-white pinny and the black dress
she always wore for her husband killed in the war.
My grandfather.
A tattered old book she always read,
verses I could not understand.
Her voice, so sweet and gentle.
No cross words passed through her lips.
Wrapped up in her shawl,
giving heat from the winter's cold air.
What a joy I had as a boy.
She would talk of God and Heaven, where she is now
and I still have her old tattered book.
The Bible she left to me.
God bless.

Norman Andrew Downie

TSUNAMI TEARS

I am Tsunami.
I weep to see the need.
I weep to see the greed.
I weep my tears of anger.
I sow my seeds of sorrow.
Tears flow and wash away tomorrow.

You are Tsunami.
Who is to blame?
Have you no shame?
You weep your tears of anger.
Those tears won't wash away your guilt,
Nor bring back the trust we built.

Richard Street

SEVEN SEAS

I sailed upon a sea of love and wisdom, finally to reach the shore
To find an island of freedom, chains holding me no more
Nature and beauty all around me, new was every sense,
touch, sight, smell, taste and sound
Great weight lifted from and within me spirit unbound

Sailed upon a sea or rage, anger and lonely bitterness
Found an island of empty wreckage, a place barren and in a mess

Sailed a sea of disillusionment and also confusion
Found an island, at least I think I did, maybe it was an illusion?

Sailed a sea of desire and of wanting, no island did I find
Let go of the desire and wanting from my mind

Sailed a sea of tears and sadness, when would the journey cease?
Finally the sea of tears came to shore on an island of rest and peace

I sailed upon a sea of love, wisdom and understanding,
again I reached the shore
Found an island of freedom chains holding me no more

Seven seas I sailed looking outward for an island to set me free
I know now like home the island has always been with me for eternity.

Jay Pacer

YOU HAVE A VISITOR

In the darkness of the corner of a gold hospice room,
Stands a tall, lonesome figure, face as pale as the moon.
Holding his long, tattered list, once again he's on time,
Punctual as the day he started, constant as a beat to a rhyme.

Standing draped in a gown as dark as his profession
His name known by all, but which few dare to mention.
He's here to do his job, here to complete his task
So don't look for pity as you feel his grasp.

Some will feel comfort like there's something they knew
Managing a smile like they've some place to go.
Others will ask pity, with a scared look on their face
Like a fox being hunted when it knows there's no race.

But one thing they share is the same inevitability
To go with this figure is nothing more than efficiency.
One day he will come and the outcome will be the same
To him you're no different, skin type or name.

So who will you be, whose look on your face?
Will he take you somewhere special or no particular place?
One thing's for more, we all have our date
Several years of experience, he's never been late.

Gary Knight

A LETTER TO ELIZABETH

(Sent to the Tower of London)

My dear Elizabeth, I wrote to you
At once when I knew, you were in the tower
For am I not always your friend, so true?
Thus will I strive to do all in my power
To plead with your father to free you now
Your jailer is mindful of his royal task
To get admission, yet I know not how.
Be patient friend, is all that I would ask
We were shocked to hear how your mother died
The king is nervous that he'll lose the throne
And needs a good wife to be at his side
Be of good cheer, your father will repent
And rue the time that in the tower you've spent.

Arthur F Mylam

CATALOGUE

Give me roses,
the finest you have, please
painted with all the colours
that the honey-dew brings.
For when the morning wakes up,
just as the midnight plunges into
its silvery pearls of stars.

Give me a song,
the most beautiful one you have please.
Made with the finest silk,
that a newborn could only sing;
for when we open our arms to
take that dive into the unknown
and out of golden powder of our mothers' hearts.

Give me just a little more time please,
to write this.
To make this order a little more memorable
if only it was timeless
If only life wasn't a catalogue of liability.

Katty King

THE SEAGULL

I saw a seagull standing there,
Stamping his feet in great despair.
All alone on the wet seashore,
I wondered what he was doing this for?

I walked along the Brighton pier
Right to the end and back to near . . .
And when I passed he was still standing there
With only the sun and salt, sea air.

I gazed and gazed at him stamping his feet
In chance he might meet a big fat worm that he could eat.
Minutes went past and at long last an
Unsuspecting worm appeared and just as
I feared the poor worm disappeared.

The gull's eye twinkled, he gave a squawk,
Cocked his head and went for a walk.

Janey French

FOR JACK

It is time for me to leave now and we must say goodbye
I know that this is hard for you, I can see you cry
You sit down beside me and take my paw into your hand
You say that you are sorry, but you must understand

My life has been a wonder, for I've had a friend like you
From the start we fit together, a foot in a well-worn shoe
All the times we shared and the memories that we made
Will be alive forever, they cannot die or fade

I've seen a lot of summers and I've slept for many nights
The Christmases we've spent together beneath the tree of lights
But my body hurts now and there is pain inside my head
I try to wag my tail for you, but it feels made of lead

I need you to be strong for me, I ask this last thing of you
Release me from this aged life, you know what you must do
I know that you feel sad, like you've let down your friend
But it is a kindness that you do me, for my pain will finally end

It is time for us to go now and you take me to the car
I know I'll not be coming back and we're not going far
It's hard for you to let me go, hard to say goodbye
But remember though I leave you now, my love will never die.

Janine Ayres

I SPY

There is a Father Christmas
I saw him in the hall
He had a doll for Mandy
And for me a real football.

I saw him kiss my mother
Then he gave her a hug
She started then to giggle
His beard she gave a tug.

This really made me angry
Or should I say quite mad
Until he started laughing
And sounded like my dad.

I crept back to my bedroom
I did not make a noise
I knew that if they saw me
I wouldn't get my toys.

Harold Lamb

THE CHRISTMAS TREE

I was quite happy where I was
Outside in the woody glade
Till people came, with shouts of glee
And brought with them - a blade.

Chop, chop, they went and down I fell
My branches swept the ground
They carried me off to their red-bricked home
And there my branches gowned.

In tinsel, candles, coloured balls
They decorated me
And changed my name from *Douglas Fir*
To handsome *Chris McTree.*

Marjorie Lamb

STOLEN

Close your eyes and open your mind
Leave all reason well behind
Hunt a little harder in your shallow head
Then look at the tears I shed.

I'm as good as gold and stupid as mud
And my eyes are red, as red as blood
Look a little deeper in your sin-soaked soul
Look for the innocence that you stole.

Here's a thought for you to chew
The people that you trust, they screw you too
You took everything and that's a lot
You gave me nothing, now it's all I've got.

You emptied my soul, just poured it away
What a funny game to want to play
You ruined my life, you are to blame
You were the petrol, I was merely the flame.

So now it doesn't matter what they say
They will never begin to help me find my way
It will never matter what was done or said
No one will take away this horror from my head.

Lucy Bradford

GOLDEN CHILD

Sunlight, golden, through the window
Creation goldens me.
My heart is encouraged to discover
The things that possibly can be.

I never knew the power of sunlight
Until it entered my inner life.
I apprehend the claiming, calm point
When all about me is in strife.

My stillness at the centre is golden,
A prism of sunlight held within,
A reflection of the infinite,
Prayer or consciousness, a way to begin.

Zoe Ainsworth-Grigg

LADY OF THE LAKE

She had bore the babe and now wanted none of it.
She held the child in arms, then thrust it into the unclear water,
not a loving gesture, but one of disgust.

Its clawing fingers thrashed about her wrists,
its muffled yelps only bubbles on the surface.
Yet to kill it unborn would've been unjust.

She had prayed and pleaded with the clergy,
for this was no natural kin of sanctified marriage of love.
This small bundle was a product of vile lust.

The water never cleansed her body,
the soap never smelled sweet or summer garden fresh again.
Harsh wind failed to dispel shame with its gust.

The struggling stopped as the baby died,
its arms lay limply by its sides, death had closed its eyes.
Now to the freshly dug earth and inevitably to dust.

She left the grave, unmarked and lonely,
rid of the reminder of that dreadful night in September.
Hell take her, rip her heart from her damned bust.

She cared little for life or death,
yet now she was free from his steel blue watching eyes.
No more childish stares full of his violent lust.

He was jailed and his son was gone now too;
she drifted back to the water's reeded edge.
She knew what to do, it was a case of *must*.

Her clothes weighed her down as she walked unerringly,
sodden and unburdened into the lake.
Her hair matted and tangled, the colour of rust.

Catherine Knapp

ELOQUENT SMILE

Freedom to choose
Evolution grows
How to soothe one's soul
From beyond the unspilled tears I do not know
Directions to which way
Dimensions to go
Magnetism pulls from the universe
Do tug at my heart strings
Play havoc in reverse
Won't let me go, of this -
I cannot see how
I cannot see why
To seek out self strength
For what - to press on
An intimate progression
Through the spirit of circumstance
It's all so cerebral
As I swish through the clutter in my head
I know this in conclusion
I am not yet dead
Too much to live for, to learn, to sense, to grow
It's not just knowledge I seek out
What's it all about
My dear, I do not know
Whilst relentless in my effort
Entangled - most emotions
Though so pure clear in view of you my dear - infinite beauty
A quest to manage them alone
Is all I wish to conquer
As the smile does form
Its eloquence shows

Bharti Ralhan

HAPPY NEW YEAR

You are thought of more warmly
Than you had ever guessed
And wished far more joy than thee
Words can express
So it's a great pleasure
When you are here
Hope you are happy
Today, tomorrow and all through the year.

Because you are you, just as nice
As anyone ever could be
Hope our relationship is twice as nice
As you ever thought it would be
And the coming year is as wonderful
And happy as it should be.

Some wishes are just for a year
But this is a fond wish for you,
Who's always so dear . . .

Arvinder Singh Chadha

DOLL

All dressed up
For fun and games

I feel like a doll

A lady should at all times
Look, move and speak like a lady

Words of wisdom

Comfort is thrown
Out of the window

I feel like a doll

Have your ever tried sitting in a corset so tight
That you can't even breathe?

I didn't think you had

Individualism
Is not a welcome factor here

I act like a doll

A lady will make a good impression,
Acting how you want is the key to my
Success

Soul destroying madness

I am surrounded by
False faces and fake smiles
Sugar-coated candied words trip
From beautiful empty plastic mouths

I love you all

Kerry Grice-Richards

THE TRAFFIC JAM

Cruising along at sixty-five
Traffic moving smoothly
Freedom of a relaxed drive
No one's behaving like a hoolie
Then your ears pick up the ringing bell
Of fire engine, ambulance or police car
Speeding services. Oh well
Nobody's going very far!

Close the windows
Don't inhale
The toxic fumes, that are stale
As you move at speed of snail
The petrol gauge is now on red
A breakdown on the motorway!
Sweat drips down, mounting dread
This isn't how it ought to be!

This is the time for rising hatred
Of drivers on hard shoulder
They are cheating to get ahead
Attitudes get colder
Cars changing lanes
Drivers jockey for position
False hopes, optimism wanes
More of this inquisition
At last the turn off comes in view
Gloom now turns to chatter
My goodness, where's that steam come from?
Now we're out of water!

Eric Jackson

BROKEN PLEDGE

A broken heart, brittle, clutches to hope
Dissolving into self pity, determined to cope
Bruised, broken, beyond repair
Wondering, hoping, waiting in despair

A mind shattered, dangling on the edge
Emotions run deep, a broken pledge
Trying to claw back pieces of self respect
To rescue sanity, time to reflect

Gradually rebuilding a confidence flawed
From spirits shattered, to a soul gnawed
Head from clouds, feet firmly on ground
For yesterday's dream, just a distant sound

From curtains of doubt, draw in the new
Step by step, gentle, a life to pursue
For experience of life can never be taught
For bitterness, hostility, life's too short.

R S Wayne Hughes

MY ANGELS

Pretty in pink, you lay in your beds,
I gently kiss your little heads.
I can't believe how perfect you both are,
Fallen from a shining star.
To us you're our gift,
Sent to give our lives a lift.
You two are obviously meant to be,
Half of daddy, half of me.
Sisters that love each other so much too,
We're so grateful for both of you.
We loved you before you were even born,
This bond of ours can never be torn.
We're so lucky to have both of you,
It's the best thing we could ever do.
With such delicate, soft, smooth skin,
You churn so much love from deep within.
There's nothing better than your baby's touch,
It's hard to believe you can love this much.
For you both I would do anything,
You make my heart want to sing.
I will always put my babies first,
With so much emotion, I'm fit to burst.
I could hold you both forever,
Such wonderful memories I will always treasure.
I promise to do my best for you,
Because no other angels deserve it more than my two.

Tania M Taylor

FOSTER CARE

Foster care is the best
Mike makes a lot of mess
But Elly always clears it up
Because she doesn't like muck.
Tasha Tasha has a cat
Someday she would like to live in a flat
Codie cat has her own warm bed
But I'm sure she would like to sleep somewhere else instead.
Elly Elly is full of care
A woman like her is extremely rare
Sometimes she says, 'On your bike!'
But I cannot say how much she loves Mike.

Daniel Edwards (10)

INFORMATION

We hope you have enjoyed reading this book - and that you will continue to enjoy it in the coming years.

If you like reading and writing poetry drop us a line, or give us a call, and we'll send you a free information pack.

Alternatively if you would like to order further copies of this book or any of our other titles, then please give us a call or log onto our website at www.forwardpress.co.uk

**Anchor Books Information
Remus House
Coltsfoot Drive
Peterborough
PE2 9JX
(01733) 898102**